D1321000

Little Pebble™

Celebrate Autumn
Apples

by Erika L. Shores

raintree
a Capstone company — publishers for children

Raintree is an imprint of Capstone Global Library Limited, a company incorporated in England and Wales having its registered office at 7 Pilgrim Street, London, EC4V 6LB – Registered company number: 6695582

www.raintree.co.uk
myorders@raintree.co.uk

Edited by Mari Bolte and Erika Shores
Designed by Cynthia Della-Rovere
Picture research by Svetlana Zhurkin
Production by Katy LaVigne

ISBN 978 1 4747 0295 9
19 18 17 16 15
10 9 8 7 6 5 4 3 2 1

British Library Cataloguing in Publication Data
A full catalogue record for this book is available from the British Library.

Acknowledgements
Alamy: Picture Partners, 21; Capstone Press: Gary Sundermeyer, 13; Capstone Studio: Karon Dubke, 7, 9, 17; Dreamstime: Dave Bredeson, 19; iStockphoto: ericmichaud, 11; Shutterstock: Christian Jung, Cover, Dancake, (dots in red line by photo) throughout, Dancake, (green apple w/ leaf) throughout, (ripe apple w/ leaf) throughout, Everything, (red apple) throughout, George Dolgikh, 15, JIANG HONGYAN, (green apple) throughout, Jirapolphoto, (water on apples) 1, 2, 22, Mega Pixel, 12, Nitr, 5, pukach, 8, Roman Samokhin, (red apple on side) throughout, SeDmi, 6

Every effort has been made to contact copyright holders of material reproduced in this book. Any omissions will be rectified in subsequent printings if notice is given to the publisher.

Printed and Bound in China.

Contents

Apple trees

Apples tell us autumn
is here!

Apple trees grow
in orchards.

Flowers on the trees are called blossom.
Blossom falls off.
Then apples grow.

apple

Picking apples

Pick the ripe apples.
A basketful is called
a bushel.

Grab one to eat.

Take a great big bite!

The apple's centre
is the core.
How many seeds
can you see?

I found six seeds
inside my apple!

16

Cut up
green apples.
Bake them in pies.

Time for a sweet

autumn treat!

Glossary

blossom flower on a fruit tree

bushel way to measure an amount of apples

orchard field or farm where fruit trees are planted

ripe ready to pick and eat

seed part that will grow into a new plant or tree

Read more

All About Seeds (All About Plants), Claire Throp (Raintree, 2014)

Food From Farms (World of Farming), Nancy Dickmann (Raintree, 2011)

Websites

www.bbc.co.uk/gardening/digin/your_space/patch.shtml
Celebrate autumn by growing and harvesting fruit and vegetables in your garden or on your windowsill. Follow the BBC's step-by-step picture guide to help you get started.

www.naturedetectives.org.uk/autumn/
Download wildlife ID sheets, pick up some great autumn crafting ideas and collect recipes for some delicious autumn cooking projects on this website.

Index